RICO LEBRUN
Mexican Fruit
Oil on panel, 36 x 52

Collection, Mr. and Mrs. Dan McFadden

2

The Realm of Contemporary Still Life Painting

Bentley Schaad

Reinhold Publishing Corporation · New York

the Author expresses deep appreciation to the Artists whose paintings are reproduced in this book

■ FIFTY-FOUR PAINTERS

COLOR PLATES ■

© 1962, Reinhold Publishing Corporation
All Rights Reserved
Printed in the United States of America
Library of Congress Catalog Card No. 62-19485
Designed by Ernest W. Watson
Type set by Howard O. Bullard, Inc.
Printed and Bound by The Comet Press, Inc.

■ CONTENTS

■ PREFACE

In writing this book, my main concern has been with the serious art student at every level of his development, whether he is experiencing for the first time the excitement of discovery in this most challenging of creative fields or whether he be the more advanced student seeking a firmer foundation on which to establish a broader basis for his continued growth as an artist.

The investigation and study of still life is vital to the development of every art student, and yet it is seldom presented in such a manner as to stir the imagination of the young artist or stimulate his desire to go beyond the narrow confines of the usual sterile classroom "setup." As a result the magnificent and limitless potentialities inherent in still life painting have rarely been explored.

One would be hard pressed indeed to find an artist of important stature who has not at one time or another turned to the drawing or painting of still life as a means of revitalizing his vision and deepening his understanding of the form life that surrounds him and enriches his existence.

Since the latter part of the nineteenth century, painting from still life as a means of study has resulted in many of the most important advancements in the growth of contemporary art. At the same time it has, perhaps, been the most abused and misunderstood of all art forms, both by the layman and the some-time painter. With few exceptions, all periods in modern art have pivoted around still life as a source for experimentation and inspiration. It is with this in mind that I welcome the opportunity of attempting to help the painting student and other art-minded people to better understand the importance of still life study as an essential basis for all painting, and to present it as a potential source for self-expression.

I have found a tendency on the part of some beginning students to shy away from the disciplines of still life study, which by their very nature involve and demand a firm grasp of all the fundamentals of drawing, painting, and design. There is a strange and inexplicable fear that this searching attitude may in some way stifle their desired goal for self-expression. Nothing could be further from the truth; I believe still life to be the natural and most practical means for developing the student's capacity for self-expression and increasing his ability to communicate. We will, therefore, be most concerned here with the basic tools of communication in painting. For if an artist has something to say, it is well that he have the means and ability to make himself understood in the most explicit manner possible.

The artist's ultimate goal must be to paint what he knows rather than being restricted merely to copying the superficial appearance of what he thinks he sees. Since this is essentially an instructive book from a technical standpoint we will, of course, concern ourselves with many of the disciplines of painting. At the same time it is my earnest desire to awaken in the student a fuller realization of the profoundly moving experience inherent in painting that can come only through complete involvement with the world around him. For unless and until an artist has begun to develop a personal philosophy in which he deeply believes and which he feels compelled to convey through the medium of his art, painting becomes a sham, or at most a meaningless decoration.

Thus, our investigation of the possibilities in still life is not to be considered as an end in itself; it will prove to be the backbone of all our work whether it involves the figure or landscape or other subject matter. It will confront us with every basic problem of drawing, painting, and composition, often in the most elementary form. Is it not obvious, for example, that if we have trouble building the simple form of an apple, we will never be able to construct a really convincing head? It must be remembered that when we are working with a figure, we are not concerned with face painting, but rather with head painting, and then only as it relates to the total structure of the body. Without this firm understanding of how to build the basic structure of the total form, we end up with merely a half shell or mask.

I have found myself when writing this book constantly thinking in terms of "building a painting" rather than simply "painting a picture," often relying upon such expressions as structure and construction, building forms and establishing touchable planes. Admittedly, this reference to still life painting in structural terms is influenced by my personal philosophy and experience, my foibles and prejudices; and yet, at no time do I wish to imply that there is only one way to paint; no more than there can be a synthetically imposed way for all to see, feel, think, or believe. What is presented here is not meant to be a final statement on "how to paint." In the last analysis, each artist must, in time, discover his own means of expression, the way he must paint becoming "the way" for him.

May I now, for a moment, turn my attention to the young student seriously contemplating entering the professional field of fine arts. When we speak through still life painting, we are after all speaking with the language of all fine arts. The essentials are the same for all, regardless of the subject matter, the media, or the individual manner of expression with which we choose to convey our concern with life and the world in which we live. The opportunities and challenges confronting the serious artist today are greater than ever before. The ability to meet the challenges demands not only sound training in the technical areas of his profession, but assumes a rich heritage, acquired through the study of the humanities and sciences, which produces a sound understanding of the artist's role and his responsibilities in the community of man. It is vital that each young professional painter be thus fully prepared to function in every aspect of our society if he is to realize his creative potential as a twentieth century man.

There are vast opportunities open to professional artist-designers capable of fulfilling the ever increasing desire for the use of fine art by individuals and the church, the business community and public institutions at every level of government. Laymen in all walks of life are awakening to a greater aesthetic awareness of the essential role art must play in the enrichment of their daily lives.

The spectacular architectural achievements being made today are often the result of bringing the artist-designer and architect together in a closer working relationship. The introduction of revolutionary structural materials and media has contributed greatly to the creative renaissance of mid-twentieth-century art, resulting in better and more extensive use of the fine arts, especially in such areas as mural painting, stained glass, and sculpture; in religious artifacts and most decorative arts in general.

At first glance this may all seem far afield from the study of still life painting. While there are many important contemporary artists who have found still life to be their most natural outlet for creative self-expression, to place this book in its proper perspective it must be recognized that the majority of students in their formal training will become involved with still life painting primarily as a source of enrichment in their total development as professional artists.

It is with this broader view in mind that I have attempted to demonstrate the importance of still life, not necessarily as a field of concentration but as an integral part of an artist's growth.   **Bentley Schaad** Jan. 1, 1962

JERRY GOSS

Shell Studies

Ink, 40 x 26

Collection of the Artist

The fundamentals of basic drawing must be considered a prerequisite to any form of instruction in painting. Drawing unquestionably is the very backbone of all painting, the essential structural underpinning upon which a truly sound painting must be built. Weak drawing simply cannot be disguised with paint no matter how thickly it is laid on or how cleverly manipulated. Any good art instructor will tell you that incompetence in drawing is the greatest single deterrent to a painting student's progress. As for the professional painter it would be unthinkable for him to be unable to draw with perception and understanding in the fullest sense of the words. This ability implies a sensitive and enquiring mind, forever eager and searching.

I place so much emphasis upon drawing at the outset because in teaching I have discovered that its importance as a fundamental in painting is not appreciated as it was when its function in traditional representational work was so obvious; when natural appearance was given, if not priority, at least prominence with design and composition, color and values. These abstract elements are often dominant today and the student naturally is eager to become involved with them and with tactile characteristics of three-dimensional form. As to the latter, one might well spend considerable study in the sculpture class where form itself is the immediate goal.

Today drawing as always takes its rightful place with all these other factors in the technique of communication through painting as an applied art. Taken all together they are the essential tools of self-expression for the truly creative artist.

But this is not the whole story. The dedicated student must recognize that these visual aspects of art mean very little without commensurate training in the liberal arts. These constitute an indispensable extension of the artist's intellectual and cultural background; their inclusion in the art curriculum helps the artist to find his rightful function in contemporary society. This need is recognized today in most of our fine art schools.

Obviously it is not possible to do complete justice to the whole realm of draughtsmanship in the limited space provided in this book, which focuses upon the problems of the still life painter. Yet the principles and attitudes inherent in any area of drawing have universal application. It should be noted that now and then every serious painter—regardless of his subject matter—refreshes himself at this source of discipline and study. When one thinks of the insatiable curiosity of truly great draughtsmen, their capacity for complete involvement in every facet of life, the genius of Leonardo da Vinci comes especially to mind. We are staggered by the seemingly infinite number of searching studies turned out in the lifetime of that inquisitive, analytical master. His artistry and his inventiveness are illustrated in many volumes but I shall mention only one—and a good one—The Drawings of Leonardo da Vinci, a fine survey edition edited by A. E. Pophman. Research of Leonardo's drapery studies alone gives an invaluable contribution to the student's still life study, in which drapery often becomes a substantial compositional element.

Study of drawings by all the great masters is, of course, imperative in the development of any serious student. Each has something unique to contribute. Rembrandt's linear drawings and composition studies of the movement of light and shadow are particularly relevant to our problem in still life painting. Cézanne, Rodin, Picasso, Kollwitz, Braque, Toulouse-Lautrec are among the great masters of European fame; Bellows, Graves, Grosz, Lebrun, Marin, Shahn are but a few names in the American galaxy of master draughtsmen. Any brief listing merely scratches the surface; the company of the great is large and their acquaintance is both an enchantment and an inspiration to the art student.

It is helpful in our study to consider drawings in three basic categories: the sketch, the composition—or investigative study—and the drawing which is executed as an end in itself, that is, a complete statement of the artist's intention and response. We will be most concerned here with drawings made for study and composition.

N. P. BRIGANTE
Still Life on the Floor
Sketch, india ink and wash, 25 x 36

JAMES MUHS
Cactus, study

JAE CARMICHAEL
Spring Bouquet
Charcoal and ink sketch

JERRY GOSS

Studies from a Magnolia
Ink, pencil and wash, 40 x 40

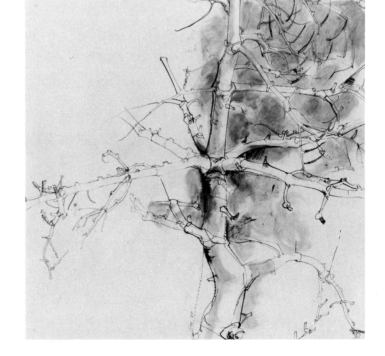

JERRY GOSS

Study of a Twig
Ink and wash, 40 x 40
Collection of the Artist

15

MORRIS BRODERSON
Roses, study
Collection, Mr. and Mrs. Richard Crenna

Sketching

A sketch is usually a linear drawing intended to capture a fleeting moment or mood. As such it is very valuable for future reference or direct use in a more ambitious study or painting. It may well be said that this type of drawing is the most demanding of an artist's skill and understanding. The student should acquire the habit of carrying a small sketch book wherever he goes: in the park, on the street, on a bus, or in the cafe; in this way recording the immediacy and the interest of life he finds around him everywhere.

The expression "it's just a sketch," often used as an excuse for a clumsy and incompetent drawing, is perhaps the most blatantly abused concept of the meaning and intent of a sketch, which, if it deserves attention at all, ought to be a useful bit of information or a serious commentary on some facet of life, no matter how casual.

RICO LEBRUN

Study for the Head of Noah

Pen and ink

Collection, Mr. and Mrs. Julius Bele

The Drawing as a Study

Study and composition drawings are of great importance to us in working with still life. For pure structural study of form I would suggest that the student investigate the possibilities in working from all kinds of nature forms: shells, plant forms, animal skeletons, and the like. He might hold them in his hand or set them on his drawing board where a very intimate searching of their structural form life can be made. Pen and ink is perhaps the most demanding medium for such study and therefore the most productive for digging out and nailing down on paper the very essence of the total structure. There is great advantage in drawing on large sheets of wrapping or butcher's paper from time to time. Pin these large sheets on a full panel of Masonite or plywood, 4 x 8 feet, or on the studio wall, and draw studies of these small forms greatly enlarged from their original size. Working big in this way prevents any possibility of being able to cover up the slightest lack of understanding of any segment in the total structure.

Composition Drawings

Composition drawings are made in anticipation of a finished painting and as such involve a greater concern with the entire picture plane, including an analysis of the over-all movement or gesture of the dark-and-light pattern as it will weave throughout the painting. It is here that we investigate as many variations of design and composition as possible. One should try doing drawings from several different positions and points of view, even looking straight down on the setup, wherein many relationships and composition possibilities will be discovered that might never have occurred to the artist in working from a conventional viewpoint.

These drawings might be comparatively small and very broad in execution, or what might amount to a sort of personal abstract shorthand that would have very little meaning to any one other than the artist himself. Working in a rapid manner, with charcoal, gives one the opportunity to try out innumerable ideas and compositions in a very short time. They may even suggest some readjustments of the setup itself.

EDGAR EWING
Homage to Darius
Courtesy Dalzell Hatfield Galleries

JAE CARMICHAEL

Wild Weeds

Composition Drawing

JACK STUCK **Composition Drawing**

Still Life
Color etching, 24 x 18

DON TURNER

Graphic Replica
Collection, Mr. and Mrs. Peter Engle

Composition Drawing

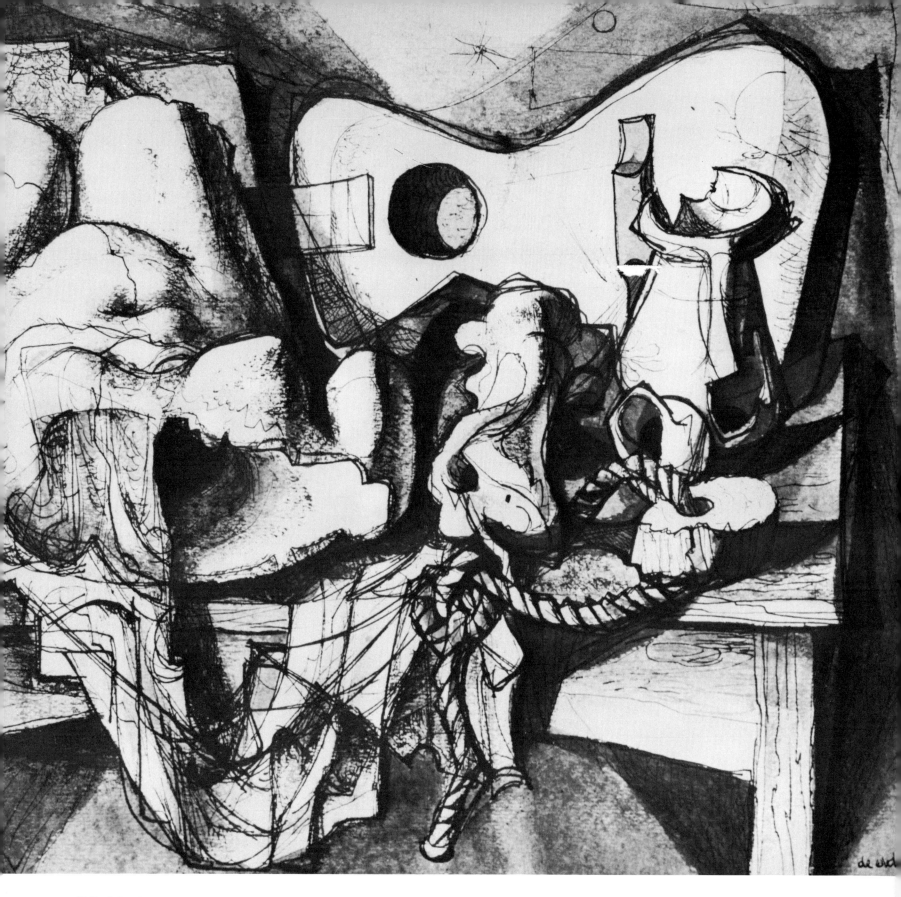

FRANCIS de ERDELY

Fragments and Fancy

Composition Drawing

ANITA H. FAHS
Untitled

Composition Drawing

One very important point to remember is always to draw out an indication of the picture plane on paper—bounded by its outline—before beginning to make any composition study; for the picture plane is our point of reference or frame of space to which we design. One should consider the possibilities of trying out both vertical and horizontal statements.

Many artists after completing these preliminary shorthand drawings move directly into the actual painting on their canvas. However, I find that it is wise for the student to carry these drawings one step further. After deciding upon the point of view or position from which he wishes to paint his still life, he might profitably make a more complete compositional study, perhaps on a sheet of paper the same size as the finished painting. If not the exact size of the painting, it should at any rate be large, perhaps a minimum of 30 x 40 inches. Use charcoal or ink washes or a combination of both to establish most effectively the overall masses of dark and light.

We may start our composition by building a linear framework, adding the masses of dark and light as the structure grows. Work as broadly as possible, with very little detail, being sure the entire picture plane grows as an entity. It is

EDWARD REEP

Old Door

Pen and ink, 22 x 12

Collection, Los Angeles County Museum

Composition Drawing

DIFFERENT COMPOSITION IDEAS IN SMALL STUDY SKETCHES

LARGE COMPOSITION DRAWING about 30 x 40
ink washes and charcoal from small studies

dark masses
with black paper

starting with
wash in three values

adding middle values
with gray paper

drawing back in
with charcoal and
pen and ink

adding charcoal,
gesso and ink washes

MICHAEL FRARY
Still Life with Fish
Collage, 35 x 48

at this stage that every portion of that picture plane must start to function in relation to the whole. For in the final analysis every square inch of the canvas is of equal importance, even though every portion of it will not be given equal emphasis in the finished painting. Still, every section of our canvas must always play its full part, regardless of how starkly simple we may wish any area to be in our completed painting.

Another excellent way of beginning a composition drawing is by starting right off with broad ink washes and painting-in the big movements and masses of dark-and-light found flowing in and out through the total setup. Try limiting yourself, in any case, to just three values: black, white, and one middle value of gray. After establishing the gestures or slabs of dark and light, draw back into the composition with pen and ink and charcoal, re-establishing the delineation of individual forms.

The Use of Collage for Composition Drawings

Still another method of creating a composition drawing is with collage. I have found this technique one that gives exceptionally fine results because it helps the student immediately and with simplicity to think in terms of shapes and mass and, at the same time, forces him to consider the total picture plane right from the very start of his drawing. Here again the work should be large and executed on a fairly firm surface, such as chip board, cardboard, or a prepared gesso panel of Masonite. I would again suggest that the student limit himself to pieces of paper of black, white, and a middle value of gray. These may be sheets of gray construction paper, but it is better to prepare one's own papers, painting them with watercolor or ink washes of black and

LUCILLE BROKAW
The Lobster
Collage, 26 x 21
Courtesy Esther Robles Gallery

29

gray. These will have a much more sensitive quality than the slick, machine-made surfaces of construction papers. To these may be added some pieces of brown wrapping paper, not only for a change of surface, but also for variation of color. I recommend using no more than two, fairly neutral, grayish colors, perhaps one warm and one cool, in conjunction with the values of gray. This kind of composition collage is intended primarily for a study of dark-and-light relationships for a future painting, not as an end in itself.

The reason for using collage as a medium is not the decoration of a surface, but the building of the over-all structure both of the forms themselves and the negative areas in the composition. By studying the setup we try to see the total shape of dark, including the dark on the positive forms and the darks in the negative areas surrounding them. We cut that total shape out of black paper and paste it on our panel. Next we look for the basic transitional gray between the darkest dark and the lightest light in the setup and establish that by pasting in the middle value of gray paper. Allow the lightest lights to remain the white of the gesso panel. Now we are ready to work back into this basic statement of lightest light, middle value, and the black of the dark shapes with charcoal, ink washes, and additional gesso if desired, in order to adjust the large gesture of light.

It is possible to continue to build a composition in this manner by constantly working back and forth throughout the collage with all of these various materials, making adjustments in the linear drawing, the building of the structure, the mass of each form, and the over-all shape of the dark and light movement throughout the total picture plane.

As one investigates the possibilities of collage, he should experiment with many types of paper and mixed media. The one point to keep constantly in mind is that collage is used as a construction or building material for the establishment of a plastic statement of space, form, and structure; not for the achievement of a purely decorative, flat pattern design.

PHYLLIS JEAN RAMSEY

Armor

Collage, mixed media on panel

BENTLEY SCHAAD
Variation #3
Collage composition, 30 x 24
Courtesy Home Savings and Loan

VARDA
Still Life
Collage composition
Courtesy Ankrum Gallery

Strain

Drape

Contraction

Direct
Transition

Interlocking
Transition

Intermediate
Transition

34

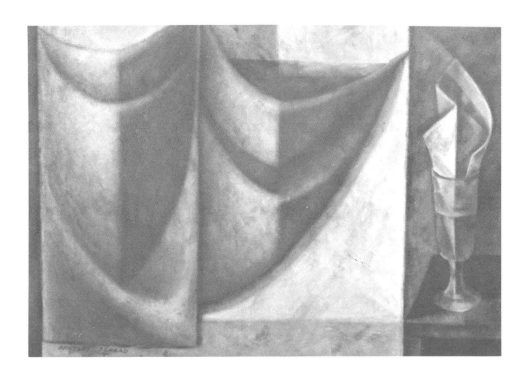

BENTLEY SCHAAD
Golden Cloth
Oil on canvas, 25 x 36
Courtesy Paul Rivas Gallery

There is seldom sufficient realization of the possibilities inherent in the use of drapery as an element of composition in painting. It seems strange indeed that students who spend a great deal of time and effort in searching analyses of a still life or a figure painting will virtually ignore the significant contribution which drapery can make to the composition if its structural and design function is understood.

In figure drawing where serious concern may be given to the anatomy and form of the model there is often almost complete neglect of the costume and drapery which contains and surrounds it. Drapery has its own anatomy, it cannot sensibly be disregarded or slighted because it echoes and enhances whatever forms it clothes. Furthermore, it can be used as a creative design element in building the pictorial statement. When it is treated in meaningless streaks of charcoal or confused slashes of paint it is worse than useless as an element in the picture's structure.

In still life the drawing and designing of drapery can have great possibilities for composition in areas of color or pattern, as a transitional structure moving through the setup, and as character and form variation. Drapery may at times become an intricate and labyrinthine structure that in its involvement enhances other more starkly simple sections and forms. Or functioning in a comparatively quiet area in rich, broad forms and planes of color it may serve as a foil or a change of pace for the more complex areas or forms.

There certainly is no obligation to use drapery in setting up a still life. Too often a great amount of material is draped all over a still life with little selectivity or the slightest concern for its eventual contribution to the final composition. Acres of elaborate brocade surrounding and submerging the beauty of a few basically simple objects can hardly be justified as a meaningful juxtaposition of form and design. In many instances the inclusion of drapery in a still life seems to be used more as a cliché device than as a necessary design element that contributes to the form life of the painting. Drapery does offer wonderful opportunity for the play of textural variations, for linear and mass movements and for design patterns. Its color masses can greatly enrich many setups.

The student should make drawings and wash studies of many different types of material, in so doing discovering that each kind of fabric has its own unique characteristics, while retaining the same basic anatomy and structural elements to be found in all drapery forms. Some material is stiff in character and falls into sharp, brittle and angular folds or planes. Some are heavy and softer; these fall into massive flowing forms, giving a feeling of weight and opulence. Still others, such as silk, are thin, with agitated shapes, often picking up light in a flashing, turbulent way.

Without attempting merely to imitate or render these various material characteristics, experiment with large drawings of each of these basic types in turn. Hang a large piece on the wall of the studio, or drape some over the back of a chair or over a table. A dressmaker's mannequin, salvaged from attic or junk shop, is a very useful prop upon which to drape material in your study of the manner in which drapery accentuates and repeats the structure of the human figure. The knowledge of the distinctive qualities of these materials may well suggest the very character of line or brush stroke one uses in expressing them. In painting the richness of a heavy, massive velvet for example, you will be likely to find yourself using broad brush strokes that flow in a ponderous, slow moving manner across your canvas or paper. The brittle quality of a stiffly starched material that breaks up into jagged, agitated forms and crisp folds will naturally be better characterized by a rapidly moving pen line, which will express its hard, structural characteristics, which may appear almost metallic in quality.

HENRY LEE McFEE
Crow with Peaches
Oil on canvas, 30 x 28
Collection Whitney Museum of American Art

A Formal Set-Up

DAVID LOEW
Still Life

A Formal Set-Up

■ BASIC FOLDS AND FORMS

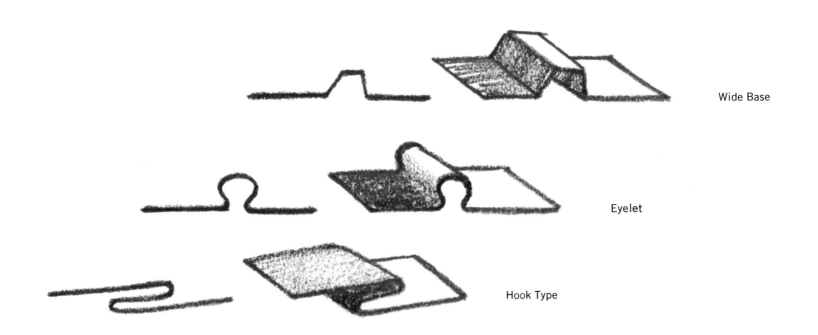

Wide Base

Eyelet

Hook Type

BASIC FORMS OF FOLDS

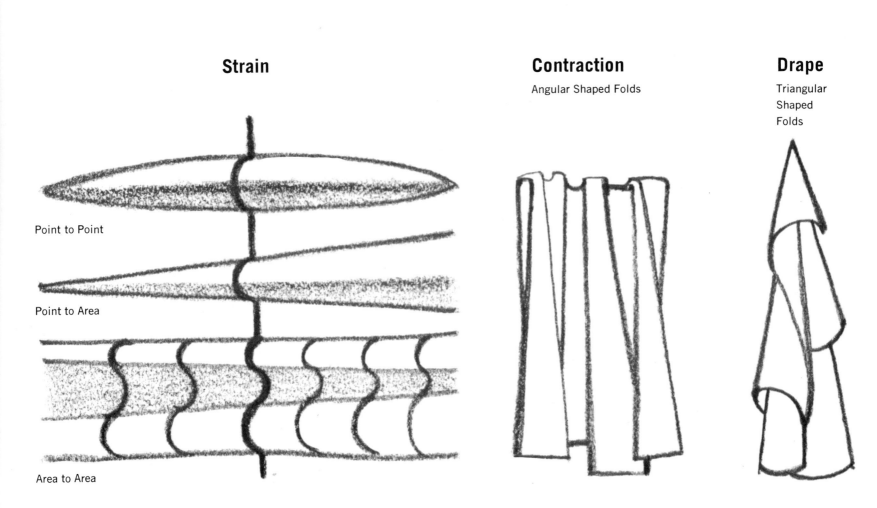

Strain

Point to Point

Point to Area

Area to Area

Contraction

Angular Shaped Folds

Drape

Triangular
Shaped
Folds

Blue Flowers
Oil on canvas, 30 x 25

Blue Table
Oil on canvas, 36 x 30

FIVE PAINTINGS BY THE AUTHOR
Courtesy Paul Rivas Gallery

Tea Pot Oil on canvas, 30 x 25

Of Things Past Oil, 36 x 30

Harvest Oil on canvas, 36 x 30

This approach should not be confused with a tight, mechanical rendering which simply results in the imitation of surface effects. As always, your personal involvement with every subject should suggest the nature of media and tools that will best serve as the most natural means of expressing each subtle character variation.

It is a good idea to select large pieces of material of one color that are without pattern (which might tend to camouflage the form) for your first drapery studies. A black or white material is excellent to start with; each presents a good opportunity to check your ability to control value relationships.

When starting a drapery study, look first for the broad gesture and movement of the total form. Search for the points of tension or stress and their cause. Note what happens to the material as it moves across the flat surface of a table top, then breaks and drapes over the edge; see how it falls from a wall as though straining in the effort to pull away from the nails from which it hangs. Try to visualize your drapery study as being primarily a sculptural problem; break it down in your mind's eye to its essential forms, planes, and folds, eliminating all of the incidental little creases and minor surface variations that do not contribute to the building of the total structure. Take full advantage of the lights and shadows as they crawl in and out and across the mountainous surface, accentuating rather than destroying the rich hills and valleys of form. Establish the extreme range of the subject's value from dark to light and then by using no more than five values, build your basic structural statement. Having thus established in sculptural terms what might otherwise have been a fairly complex form, it is comparatively easy to work back into your study, digging out whatever subtle variations help to describe the singular characteristics of the particular material you are painting.

Once a student has discovered the potentialities of actually building drapery as a design and structural element in composing a painting, it is doubtful that he will ever again be satisfied with the vague and mushy areas of pigment which too often are made to pass for drapery.

HENRY LEE McFEE
Still Life: Green Fruit
Courtesy City Art Museum of St. Louis

BENTLEY SCHAAD
Every Man's Castle
Oil on canvas, 40 x 25

Using the Value Scale In Painting

Light and dark rendering, although not always necessary, is quite valuable in building form. When working with light and shadow we must also consider the problem of value, or what is often called "tone." I use the term value in preference to tone; it is a more explicit and less confusing expression. Value refers to the relative lightness or darkness of a color or of a gray in the full value scale, ranging from black to white. Therefore, if we say a color or a gray is low or dark in value, we mean it is nearer the black end of the value scale; if high or light in value, it is closer to the white end of the value scale.

The ability to recognize and control the use of values is of vital importance in painting as well as in drawing, for color and value should work hand in hand. Oftentimes a student will think he is having trouble with color when in reality his problem is primarily a lack of understanding of the function of value and of value relationships. Many painting students, even those who are comparatively advanced, have a difficult time recognizing the value of a color, and its relationship to other factors within the entity of a painting. This naturally proves to be a stumbling block until they have developed sufficient sensitivity to value relationships to make fine distinction between even subtle differences. It is not enough to recognize that a color or an area is dark or light, the problem is, rather, how dark or how light, how dark it is in relationship to true black, how light when related to true white.

We are constantly confronted with this concern for color values whether we happen to be working with an objective painting, an abstraction or even a completely non-objective statement; the instant we put a note of color or gray on a white canvas, we are immediately dealing with value. The problem of values and value relationships is not restricted to the representation of an artificial or a natural light source

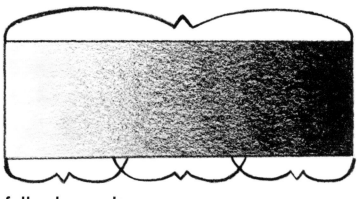

full value scale

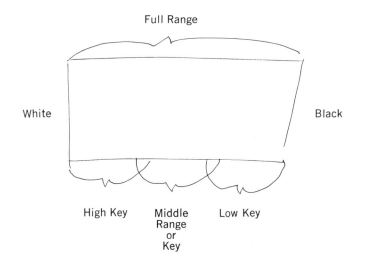

Full Range

White   Black

High Key   Middle   Low Key
            Range
            or
            Key

high key—white to middle gray

low key—black to middle gray

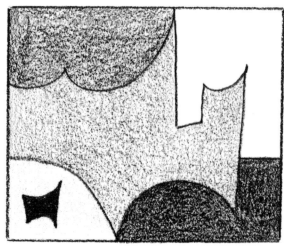

full key range—black to white

**middle key
central range of the value scale**

VALUE STUDIES

extreme value range

transitional grays added

completed full value scale

Fig. 1.

Fig. 2.

Fig. 3.

as it plays upon our subject matter, it also applies to light and dark color areas that may move throughout a non-objective painting having nothing to do with light and shadow in the literal sense. The desire here may be simply to create a movement or a pattern of dark and light shapes that will function independently of the color pattern.

It is not necessary or desirable in every painting to use the full value scale of white to black, as for example when we are executing what is called a high-key painting. In such a painting, all of the color values in the picture are located in the upper range, that is, near the white end of the value scale. In a low-key painting we use color values that fall in the lower range or black end of the value scale. Thus we may develop a successful painting by using the entire value range or we may confine it to any section of the scale we desire just as long as we maintain a consistency of value relationship throughout the picture. Arbitrary and inconsistent use of value changes in a painting will cause the picture to appear spotty and fall apart. It can even take on the appearance of a checkered board or of a confused, all-over pattern.

Working with a limited value range either in high-key or low-key painting requires a great degree of understanding and experience in the control of the subtle value relationships that will be involved. It is therefore advisable for a beginning student or for anyone having trouble recognizing values to do large drawings in masses of dark and light from a simple setup in black, white and various gray objects. Charcoal or india ink washes are suitable for such studies. Several black, white and various gray pieces of construction paper may be incorporated in the setup, placed on the table top and pinned to the wall of the background.

The setup should be placed near a comparatively strong light source so as to create a fairly obvious, full range of values moving throughout the entire group. A good first step **(Fig. 1.)** is to allow the white of the paper to represent the lightest areas in the setup, at the same time to establish inclusively the extreme dark or gray areas that most closely approximate the black of the value scale and so, logically, to be considered as equivalent. These darkest areas, of course, may not necessarily be true black in the

Building with Light and Dark

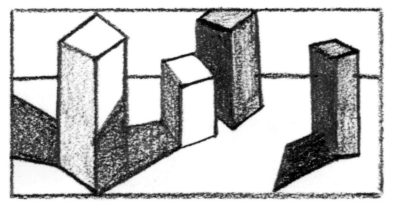

black and white objects under equal light

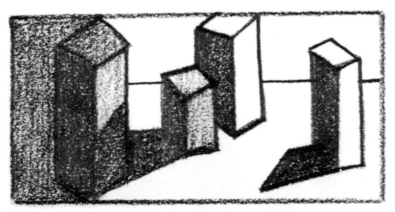

**black objects
in light and white objects in shadow**

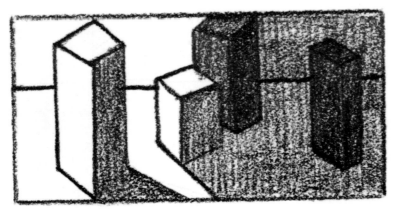

**light object
in light and dark object in shadow**

HELEN LUNDEBERG
Interior with Mirror
Collection of the Artist

setup or in the drawing. The next step would be to isolate the gray areas **(Fig. 2.)** nearest middle gray of the value scale. In this manner we are able immediately to establish the full value range as it exists in our still life. We now know that all of the other grays must fall somewhere between these extremes. By eliminating all of the small and more incidental details, it is comparatively simple to continue the building of our still life in all of its variations, constantly comparing each new gray we add with the three basic values that have already been established, and by judging just how dark or light they should be in relation to each other, as in **Fig. 3.**

After having solved several such value problems, using charcoal or ink washes as recommended and working from a basically black, white, and gray setup, the student will be more ready to move on to the far more complex study which involves the translating of a full-color still life into its true value range in terms of gray, black, and white. In this study oil paint should be used; our color palette restricted to black, white, cobalt blue, and burnt sienna. These four colors may be intermixed in any way in order to arrive at the desired value of gray. By cross-mixing these four colors it is possible to create a large number of dark, light, warm, cool, and neutral grays in the full value range. There is one important restriction that must be kept in mind in mixing these four colors; no matter how warm or cool a gray is mixed, it must in these studies be thought of as value rather than color. We are studying values, not color.

At this point I might suggest that if it is wished to mix a cool gray or black from these four pigments, more cobalt blue should be added to the mixture; if it is to be a warm gray or black, use more burnt sienna. A neutral gray may be had by mixing almost equal amounts of cobalt blue and burnt sienna with white or black. It is a good idea, before beginning the value painting, by cross-mixing on the palette to see how many variations of gray are possible from just these four colors.

LORSER FEITELSON

Untitled

Oil on canvas, 25 x 30

Courtesy Paul Rivas Gallery

BENTLEY SCHAAD

Studio Corner

Oil on canvas, 30 x 25

Collection, Mr. and Mrs. Leroy H. Hines

CLINTON ADAMS

The Cabinet

Lithograph

Courtesy Landau Gallery

CLINTON ADAMS

Emergence and Dissolution

Oil and tempera on canvas, 28 x 38

Courtesy Landau Gallery

It would be possible to solve this problem by using only black and white paint; but by including cobalt blue and burnt sienna a far greater number of subtle gray variations can be mixed and a more sensitive painting created. By the employment of color the student will more quickly develop an appreciation of the beauty of grayed colors and their limitless possibilities in painting. The use of black and white alone in a painting of this nature produces a very cold, metallic appearance that is not desirable.

The kind of painting we are discussing should be started in much the same way as the charcoal and wash value drawings already described. The great difference here being the necessity of analyzing the color in the still life and translating it into its correct values of gray. The use of a warm or a cool gray pigment is determined by the particular color in the setup which is to be translated, whether it be warm or cool. For example, a dark, warm red in the still life will become, in the painting, a dark, warm gray of the same value. Here again it would be well to establish the lightest lights, the darkest darks and the middle values as soon as possible. And as with the charcoal studies, proceed to build the intermediate gray values using these three basic values as guide posts or points of reference.

Be sure not to become tricked into assuming that a black object is always very dark or that a white object is always light. A black or white form will vary in value depending upon its relative position to the light source and to the value of surrounding objects and planes. It is quite possible for a white form or a plane to be so deep in shadow as to appear almost black. In theory, if there were an absolute lack of light, these objects would be black. It is also true that a black form or plane under a strong light may appear to be a very light gray. Keeping these phenomena in mind, it is obvious that a white form can appear as dark, value-wise, as a black form in the same setup.

Understanding this helps one to recognize that the local or actual color of a form or plane will not in itself determine the value of that form or plane. The values of all of the colors in a still life group will be dependent upon the light

BENTLEY SCHAAD
Still Life with Black Leaves
Oil on canvas, 30 x 36

environment. Several different colors, side by side under the same amount of light, may well be identical in value, separated only by their color difference. On the other hand, identical colors may differ in value when differently lighted.

In spite of these differences in color relationships due to light influences, there is no condition in normal lighting which will disguise the true color of any object. A red box will not suddenly become a blue box or a black box when seen in the shadow plane, nor will it ever appear to be a yellow box or a white one in bright light. The local color of the red box will never lose its red character regardless of the variation of its hue under different light conditions. No matter how dark the cast shadow upon a colored object it will not destroy the identity of that object's color, although it modifies its color. The problem of maintaining local color in light and shadow is more fully discussed in the chapter that deals with painting in full color.

Most students find considerable trouble with the value problems we have been discussing in this chapter but they can be overcome through persistent self-discipline. While this type of study does entail an arduous intellectual workout, it will be found well worth the effort. After solving several studies of this nature, one of the most common and troublesome problems in all of the fundamentals of painting will have been overcome. Having a firm control over value and value relationships, pasty, chalky, or washed-out looking paintings and those having a murky, muddy quality should be a thing of the past.

A convincing way of proving what one has learned by the disciplines recommended above is to repeat in full color one of the still life setups formerly done in black, white, cobalt blue, and sienna as a value study. This painting may be done either on a fresh canvas or right on top of the original gray value study after it has dried thoroughly. The student is sure to find the richness and quality of his color to have improved remarkably. With the more effective control of light and dark that has been achieved, his drawings and composition drawings will display more authority and have more clarity of meaning as preliminary studies for future paintings.

Formal Set-ups

FRED SEXTON
Still Life with Bugle and Violin   Oil on canvas, 18 x 32   Courtesy Los Angeles County Museum   Gift of Mrs. Marion H. Pike

BENTLEY SCHAAD
Plant Structure
Oil on canvas, 30 x 40
Courtesy Paul Rivas Gallery

■ THE STILL LIFE SET UP

PICTURE PLANE
(Surface of Canvas)

It is easier for some to visualize the picture containing space as a rectangular solid from which the negative space has been scooped out around the objects as in sculpture. This may make the negative space more tangible and vital as a compositional factor.

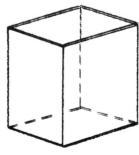

OBJECTS CONTAINED
IN SPACE

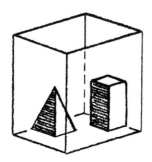

Most still life setups may be said to break down into two main sources: 1, the formal or controlled setup, and 2, the informal setup which may be considered a response to an immediate experience. When working with the so-called formal setup we have greater personal control of its basic design structure. We select objects for the interest in form, color, texture, and pattern, and we try out various lighting effects. We spend some time experimenting with the grouping of the elements, adjusting and arranging them as effectively as possible before we even begin our composition drawings. Our physical contact with the objects themselves is of great value inasmuch as we immediately become personally involved with them and with the total setup. In simply picking up an object and handling it we become more vividly aware of its tactile quality, its weight, its volume, and other individual characteristics.

In the formal setup we have control also of the negative areas that surround the objects weaving in and out throughout the entire setup. We therefore are able not only to control the relationship of the tangible forms to one another but also to relate them to the volume of space that surrounds them. We should become aware that we are dealing with a kind of space that is tangible, that has a structural use in our design. This in contrast to so-called atmosphere which is intangible, vacuous, and not constructive in our effort of building the total structure or form life of our canvas.

In painting space instead of atmosphere we are able to maintain the integrity of the picture plane (the two-dimensional surface or plane of our canvas). We control the exact depth of space extending from the surface of the picture plane back into the clearly defined limits of the picture's most distant touchable plane. This may be more clearly illustrated by visualizing our canvas as a cube of space instead of a flat surface. Its dimensions may be any size or depth we wish to establish for the building of our painting. This construction of space may be accomplished in many ways as will be illustrated and explained in future chapters. However, in the main, we will be dependent upon value relationships, color relationships and to some extent perspective. Bear in mind that still life need not be restricted to the limits of a table top setup. There is no reason why a still life may not be the painting of a single object held on the palm of one's hand, or the painting of a part of a room interior.

We now come to the informal setup, the other main source for a still life. This is what I have referred to as the response to an immediate experience. We may enter a room or our studio and discover a group of objects that have been grouped together in a somewhat casual or accidental manner, perhaps in an incongruous manner. Such accidental arrangements sometimes present most unusual and challenging compositions in their unique relationships. The inherent design structure in such a setup has a certain advantage; it offers a composition that is not too contrived or self-conscious as sometimes happens in a controlled setup. Here the painter will find surprising relationships of color, form, space, and values which it is doubtful would ever occur to him in the conscious act of setting up a still life. He comes upon a completely new experience, a fresh point of view; he is prevented from forever imposing himself so completely upon his source that his composition and design sense become proconceived and formalized. In the accidental subject we discover subtle relationships that could never be contrived or for that matter improved upon. Both of these sources for a still life painting, the formal and the informal, are equally valid; each has its own distinct advantages. In neither case, however, would we hesitate to make whatever adjustments seem necessary in our composition drawings, and subsequently in our painting, to help us achieve the finest possible relationships and in the end a more fully realized statement.

The Selection of Subject Matter
We should, of course, be highly selective about the character of objects used in a still life. It is advisable not to use objects that are so elaborately decorative or opulent in character that they tend to take on too much importance in themselves. Select objects that are free of embellishment, objects that are beautiful because of their simplicity and at the same time give the artist more freedom for his own enrichment of the whole. More about this later.

Consider carefully the number of objects chosen for constructing a setup. Again, by being selective and using fewer pieces, each form has a greater chance to live and play a greater part within the over-all form life of the composition. An overly elaborate setup, comprising many decorative forms and an extreme use of cascading torrents of drapery, takes on the character of a drug store window and becomes an intricate jumble of forms which tend to cancel themselves out, resulting, at best, in an over-all pattern. We still dis-

JAMES FULLER
Black Plant
Oil on canvas, 40 x 36
Courtesy Los Angeles County Museum
Junior Art Council Purchase Award

Informal Set-up

cover later on a similar need for selectivity in the use of color, values, textures, and abstract shapes. In the final analysis it may be said that what is left out of a painting is as important as what is put into it.

Unless the artist has a vital and truly meaningful statement to make through the juxtaposition of related subject matter, it is always well to avoid what may be considered story telling by assembling obviously related objects within an illustrative concept. Even so, it is inevitable that the spectator will read a personal meaning based upon his own experience into every painting. This may be desirable if for no other reason than it affords him the gratification of participation.

In selecting objects to be used in a still life, our main objective should be the interplay of relationships through repetition and variation of form to form, space to form, color to color associated with the play of light and dark throughout the whole. We are also concerned with scale relationships—that is, the relative size of one shape or form to another—and in addition to all of these, the functioning of textures and patterns.

An excellent setup, purely from the standpoint of a study painting, is one that encompasses many different objects and materials of varying color and textural qualities. Consider for example the contrasting textures of a glass bottle and a building brick; the one smooth and transparent, the other rough and porous in character. Compare the soft, flowing movement of drapery with the brittle quality of a wrinkled piece of paper. The inclusion of fruit contributes still another form character and affords a fine opportunity for still greater variations and subtleties of color.

HOWARD WARSHAW
Wrecked Automobiles
Gouache, 32 x 56
Courtesy Los Angeles County Museum
Purchase Prize—1949 California
Centennial of Art Exhibition

Informal Set-up

ROGER KUNTZ

Cinzano
Courtesy Felix Landau Gallery

Informal Set-up

JAMES GRANT
Still Life
Courtesy the Pasadena Art Museum

Informal Set-up

While this highly contrived selection might be made primarily for use as study material, it is well to keep in mind that we are concerned with these varied qualities to some degree in every picture we paint, whether it be a literal statement, an abstraction, or a completely non-objective work.

While we are never interested in the mere rendering of the superficial surface of anything, an awareness of possible variations in ways of handling paint helps us to appreciate and develop more sensitive paint quality in our work. At first, by necessity perhaps, an attempt at building a more painterly surface will have a somewhat self-conscious quality. In time, as awareness and a sense of response to subject matter have developed, the ability to express, and even enhance its essence, will increase and become perfectly natural. It is this kind of painterly response that transcends

**JAE
CARMICHAEL**

Yellow Apples
Casein, 40 x 30

Informal Set-up

PIERRE SICARD

Perspective

Informal Set-up

the stifling restriction of merely copying or rendering the façade of each object in the setup as an isolated entity without regard to the innate quality of each and its proper function as an integral part of the whole.

There can be no question as to the necessity for the student to acquire a firm grasp and control of his craft. But craftsmanship without expression or artistry is of little merit. It is sensuous perception that distinguishes an artist and sets him apart from the painter of pleasing pictures. Only through complete involvement with the source—his subject matter—and in turn with the act of painting will he attain that goal. The involvement I speak of is attained only when the artist acquires such an intimacy with his subject that he literally becomes one with it.

EDWARD REEP

Trappings
Oil on canvas, 48 x 36
Courtesy Paul Rivas Gallery

Informal Set-up

SHIRL GOEDIKE
Still Life with Chair
Oil on canvas, 50 x 40

Collection of Mr. Rock Hudson

Informal Set-up

The Source for Still Life Material

It is the habit of painters to collect objects that have personal meanings and to surround themselves with them in their studios. The objects I collect have no great monetary value but they have touched me in some manner and over a period of time have almost become like old friends. It often helps me to keep these props for as long as a year or more before using them in a painting, or until I have acquired a better understanding of their intrinsic nature and form life.

There are many obvious sources for finding still life material. The student may discover that his friends will welcome him with open arms if he volunteers to help clean out their attic or garage. Junk shops are likely to yield some quite magnificent props at very little expense. In a walk along the shore one can pick up such fine subjects as shells, driftwood, glass floats, and all manner of flotsam. In the vacant lot next door there may be a beautiful section of tree trunk having great structural interest.

When seeking out still life material, the sky's the limit. Why not use a suit of armor, or various sections of one? How about parts of an old automobile, or a group of dress mannequins set up as a figure composition? Or perhaps a stack of bricks of various kinds and sizes? What about the hand wringer from an old washing machine, or the whole machine, for that matter? Perhaps you can find an old sewing machine, a magnificent prop! Study all kinds of plant forms, particularly those having an interesting structural nature. Build up a stack of old chairs and tables into a labyrinthine structure. Hold a plant section or a shell in your hand and later do a painting of it fifty times its original size. Have you ever really looked at the sections of an artichoke or a pomegranate? Have you seen a whole stalk of green bananas with the blossom still attached?

KERO ANTOYAN

White on White

Collection of the Artist

Group together as many different sizes, colors, and shapes of bottles or blocks of wood as you are able to find. Try to locate and paint a skeletal section from some bird or animal. Suppose you hang up just one piece of drapery and paint that, or paint a combination of any of such objects as I have mentioned. Set them on a chair, under a table, or on a window sill; hang them from the ceiling, or set them on the floor. Who is there to say that a still life must remain within the confines of a table top?

If you haven't experimented with some of these props and discovered their possibilities, you should. The few objects I have mentioned are only suggestions, they merely scratch the surface. Try pinning many different pieces of colored paper or drapery on a wall and painting the abstract designs and patterns they create. And then for a change of pace you can always try painting just a few pieces of fruit on a table.

If a student will only investigate some of these fascinating objects and discover their rich design structures, observe their play of shapes and forms, and consider the multitude of compositional variations they suggest, he will find an entire new world of possibilities has been opened for him. Confronted with some of the unfamiliar forms and unusual

EDWARD REEP

Wicker Patio

Oil on canvas, 37 x 46

Courtesy Paul Rivas Gallery

Informal Set-up

shapes within these objects, he will discover a remarkable improvement in his sense of design and his ability to compose as he makes the effort to search them out and put them to work for him in the building of a painting.

Studio Light and the Lighting of Still Life

There are two main sources of light for studio painting: artificial and natural daylight. Many artists feel that the ideal studio lighting is a natural north light from a skylight. For several reasons, however, most professional artists must rely on artificial lighting to some extent. Artificial light is not completely satisfactory, although in recent years technical advances in the manufacture of different types of lighting have given us a very close approximation to daylight. It always requires a certain amount of experimentation to arrive at the lighting which serves best. This depends upon the physical characteristics of the artist's studio. An equal mixture of warm and cool fluorescent light tubes is usually quite satisfactory. Similarly, I have discovered that a mixture of about equal amounts of natural and artificial light functions best for the manner in which I paint.

When you begin to exhibit your work it is important to remember that most art galleries today have only artificial light. The use of a spotlight is not recommended either for figure or still life painting. Using such a light on a setup will, of course, accentuate the modeling of forms through emphatic contrasts of dark and light and may have a temporary study value for the beginner. However, it is impractical for actual painting for several reasons. For one thing, it will bleach out the richness of local color in highlights and also destroy most of the saturation of color in the shadows. An artificial light of this nature will almost certainly result in a phoney looking painting that tends to be synthetic and theatrical in character. Because of this tendency to destroy the full saturation of the true local color of an object, I would never recommend the use of a spotlight for painting.

EJNAR HANSEN

Still Life with Quince
Collection of the Artist

Formal Set-up

JAN STUSSY

A Reminder
Lacquer, 30 x 40
Courtesy Esther Robles Gallery

Using Skeletal Forms

JAN STUSSY
Leafing Plant
Oil, 30 x 40
Courtesy Esther Robles Gallery

Using Plant Forms

JACK ZAJAC
Easter Goat #1
Oil, 42 x 67
Courtesy Felix Landau Gallery

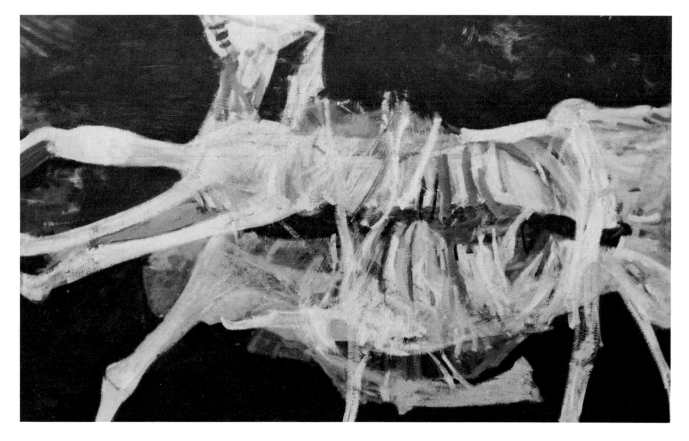

Using Skeletal Forms

First Composition Drawing

Second Composition Drawing

**Linear Wash Drawing on Canvas
Suggested areas of light and dark**

**Establishing simple notations of
local color and basic values**

■ THE BEGINNING OF A PAINTING

Laying-in a Canvas

After having completed his investigative studies and composition drawings, the student is ready to enter into the truly vital experience of painting. The laying-in of a canvas is of immense importance and will determine to a great extent the success or failure of the finished painting. It is now that every facet of training, understanding, and sensitivity must be brought into play in striving for the immediacy of his total involvement with subject matter, and in conveying to a canvas surface his response to that experience. His primary objective at this point is to establish as soon as possible the total concept of the entire picture plane. Emphasis should now be placed upon building the foundation for the final pictorial structure. The greatest danger facing a student is becoming bogged down by painting piecemeal, in isolated areas, instead of visualizing the canvas as an entity that somehow, in all its many complexities, must become a unified concept. His drawing, composition, color, and light and shadow must now all start to function as a unit and begin to mesh as a tightly integrated over-all statement.

It would be wise to re-emphasize at this point the importance of being concerned with every square inch of the canvas, even though, as stated before, we will not give equal emphasis to every segment in the final painting. Time and time again I find this lack of total concern to be the one greatest weakness many students have in composing a painting. It may help more fully to appreciate the interdependence of all elements in a composition to compare it to a house of cards which will fall apart unless each element plays its part as a supporting member of the structure.

While it is physically impossible to paint every area of a picture at the same time, it is possible to move rapidly over all the surface of your canvas, attempting to anticipate the relationship of each statement you are making to the next area to be painted and considering how each will influence and in turn be influenced by the other. In this manner one is in a very real sense constantly painting the total picture plane.

Drawing as a First Step in Laying-in a Canvas

Most artists begin their painting on canvas by drawing in one manner or another. There are some who will work out a very complete and highly controlled drawing directly with charcoal on their canvas. Some draw with a brush and a thin wash of oil paint. Still others may "draw-in" large masses and planes with a sizable brush using few lines, if any, to establish the painting's basic structure.

Students should learn to handle the brush as a drawing tool and begin a painting with a bristle brush no smaller than a No. 7, using a thin mixture of oil paint as a drawing medium.

Lacking self-confidence, some beginning students have a fear of drawing with a brush; they feel more comfortable starting work on canvas with a charcoal drawing. In their hesitancy they will invariably draw much too tightly, becoming overly concerned with many incidental details and end up with a mere tint of this very static drawing. No preliminary drawing for a painting should ever be allowed to become so tightly set and precious that there is no room for constant adjustments. The drawing and painting should be given a chance to grow, to develop in a perfectly natural manner, as the artist seeks to find still finer relationships of form, line, and mass.

For the preliminary drawing of the canvas I would suggest a mixture of cobalt blue and burnt sienna thinned down to the consistency of water-color with a medium of rectified turpentine. The advantage of using these two oil colors for drawing is that one can immediately suggest warm and cool as well as light and dark, even while still dealing in purely linear terms. This drawing should be done directly from the setup, and not be a copy of whatever composition drawing you have previously worked out. For here again spontaneity based on understanding is of the utmost importance if the painting is to grow as a living expression of the artist's intimate experience with his subject. When using this thin wash drawing as a lay-in, the artist is able to move freely throughout his canvas, constantly making subtle adjustments. At the same time he may start in very broad terms to suggest areas of light and shadow as they assist him in the building of form. He may also establish the basic gesture of the light and dark areas as they flow throughout his picture plane.

There is no need for making "erasures" of any kind; it is a very simple matter to redraw over an area that requires a slight adjustment or variation. If one finds that he has got into serious trouble in some large area, it is quite easy to rub that section out with a rag wet with a small amount of turpentine.

One of the greatest advantages of drawing as described is that it provides a very natural transition from the act of drawing into the actual start of the painting. The artist is able to move immediately right into his color painting without the feeling that "now I have finished drawing and I must start painting it." This mechanical attitude will have been entirely avoided and the artist will be able to move continuously from the drawing into painting without the slightest break in the continuity of his emotional involvement with his subject.

The Introduction of Color in the Lay-in of a Canvas

Having made a linear wash drawing upon the canvas, establishing the basic structure and over-all composition, the student is ready to move immediately into the use of color as a cohesive element that not only enhances and enriches the painting but at the same time contributes to the solidity of the whole as a statement of form and mass in space. The range and character of colors selected for the painting should express the uniqueness of the particular subject matter in all of its subtleties and relationships, and also help to establish the mood or atmosphere in which the subject lives and has its being. It is here that the clear distinction can be made between what I prefer to call **functional** color as opposed to color that is merely surface decoration. To be truly meaningful color must play a very real part in the establishment of a fully realized concept as the artist builds toward his ultimate statement in paint.

With color one is able to build both forms and space. The student will discover that he composes with color as it moves and flows throughout his painting. He will be able to draw upon his knowledge of color psychology as a means of stimulating the spectator's emotional and intellectual response. Color becomes functional when it is conceived as enrichment rather than surface decoration. A good part of the problem therefore is to put color to work for us immediately as we begin the laying-in of a canvas.

With a comparatively thin wash and a fairly big bristle brush the artist proceeds rapidly to establish large color areas. By starting the lay-in with thinned pigment he avoids a heavy impasto that would seriously hamper or prevent the controlled freedom that is so important in the building process. He needs to be free to make changes throughout the building of the painting. Painting is always difficult enough without the added problem of fighting a weak lay-in, which is, after all, the very foundation of the picture. If the start is made with an impasto it will have to be scraped off before the painter can continue with the development of the canvas, which involves continuous re-evaluation and modification. When, during later stages of painting, the canvas has become fairly heavy with pigment it may become necessary to scrape it down to the original lay-in if significant changes are contemplated. It is not wise at this stage to attempt the salvage of a poorly conceived statement.

However, a word of caution may be given here, for the scraping off of a painting frequently becomes a crutch for failure at the outset to face up to inevitable decisions and critical adjustments necessary and inherent in all creative painting. On the other hand I would not suggest for one moment that a student destroy a painting simply to avoid making a decision or attempting to solve a difficult problem. Fear or hesitancy has never spawned a successful painting.

The introduction of color to the lay-in at this point will, by its character and richness, set the pace for the final pictorial statement. In seeking out the full range of color inherent in his still life, the student painter will discover that the purest color, that is, the color that comes nearest to the true local color of an object or area, will appear somewhere in the half light. By local color I mean of course the object's actual basic color at its greatest point of color saturation. Having discovered this he will also note that the local color of an object tends to vary or to be modified as it moves either into strong light or into the shadow areas. However, it is imperative that the influences of light and shadow must never be allowed to destroy one's sense of the true local color of the total object, no matter how light or dark an object may become in the light and shadow areas, or how much that object may vary from warm to cool. For example, a red apple will not become a weak, pasty white in the light—this includes the highlight as well—nor will it become dead, muddy, or black in the shadow. Neither will this same red apple become a yellow apple in the light, nor a green apple in the shadow. Regardless of the extent of light and dark or warm and cool, and in spite of any other influences which may impinge upon this red apple, we must always retain its true color identity throughout its total form.

BENTLEY SCHAAD

Completed Painting
Oil on canvas, 30 x 24

BENTLEY SCHAAD

Still Life
Collection of Tupperwar Art Fund Fellowship

Formal Set-up

BENTLEY SCHAAD

Black Table
Oil on canvas, 30 x 36
Courtesy Paul Rivas Gallery

Architectonic Composition

This is a point that cannot be over-emphasized, for I have found that almost all students have the greatest trouble in this basic area of seeing and understanding color. Mastering the fundamental problem of maintaining this sense of local color will do more for the development of one's ability to see and handle color than all of the involved theories and color formulas combined. Keeping this importance of local color in mind, one will do well to move constantly throughout the lay-in of his painting, establishing simple notations of the purest colors as they appear in the half-light areas of all the forms and planes making up the total composition, at the same time making value notations that establish the full range of the darkest darks and lightest lights as they appear in color. By moving all over his composition, noting these basic local colors and values, the student will be able, in a short time, to construct a rich and fundamentally sound foundation upon which his painting can continue to build.

During this period of the lay-in it is only necessary to make reasonable approximations of each color and value; it is not possible to hit every color exactly until the entire canvas has been covered and the artist is able to make comparative adjustments. He should make a notation of what he feels to be the basically true color and then immediately move on to the next color statement. With more experience he will discover that he will be able to come closer each time to the right decision. As his discrimination improves he will be progressively better able to anticipate all of the colors of the total painting while his canvas is still in the lay-in stage.

Continuing constantly to move throughout his painting, he should now start to introduce the transition colors and values that serve more fully to enrich and round out the form and structure as it exists in space.

Building Toward the Completed Painting
Up to this point in our painting instruction we have been concentrating upon the problem of establishing, in a broad and rapid manner, the over-all gesture of the artist's composition, making basic notations of the dark and light movement, the local color relationships, and the extreme range of its fundamental values. It has been our effort to cover the entire canvas, placing emphasis upon building the total picture plane as an entity. It is not until we have completely covered the canvas with these essential notations, eliminating almost entirely all of the white of the original ground, that we move from the laying-in process to truly beginning to paint.

It will be noted that here again we have made a concerted effort to deal with the over-all canvas—I keep repeating this—never allowing ourselves to become trapped into painting sections or individual objects piecemeal. One of the student's greatest hazards is trying to build a painting by finishing one area or form at a time, ignoring the rest and forgetting the interdependence of each to the others. This piecemeal concept will always result in failure and can develop into a formula or habit which will be extremely difficult to overcome. Every act of drawing, composing, and painting should be one of searching for variations of relationships, either in contrasts and/or similarities throughout the total form life of the canvas. We must seek out and take full advantage of these variations in all their subtle relationships.

Now as the student proceeds to build his painting beyond the lay-in stage, the subtle adjustments in the composition, drawing, color and value relationships will become more and more demanding of his understanding and he will enter into one of the most exciting and challenging aspects of creative painting.

It is always beneficial to keep color mixtures simple, not only while working with the lay-in, but throughout the development of the painting. There are very few colors that cannot be arrived at by mixing no more than three given colors from one's basic palette. The student painter will perhaps be surprised at the many variations he is able to mix by the use of no more than any two colors. The range of colors made possible by intermixing any combination of two or three colors in addition to white is almost limitless. The surest way to destroy color, to create muddy or nondescript color, is by needlessly over-mixing too many colors when two or three are probably enough. The few colors that one will not be able to mix are the strong dye-like colors such as alizarin, thalo green, thalo blue, and the like. These are magnificent colors of great staining power and when their unique quality is indispensable are worth having in one's paint box, but they will not serve as substitutes for the colors of a basic palette. Alizarin crimson, you will notice, I would include as part of a basic palette, though not as a substitute for the cadmium reds.

In striving to enrich the color of his painting the artist will be concerned not only with its value and local color, but also with its truly unique character. This involves the recognition and use of warm and cool colors as well as the degree of grayness and intensity of each color in his still life. And here again these variations are relative.

It is not sufficient simply to recognize that a color is red. He must now determine in what manner it is different from or similar to all the other reds in his still life. What are the influences under which it exists? Where does this red live in relation to the light source? Is it in the shadow or in a half-light area? In what position is it in space relative to his picture plane? To what extent is the importance of this area of red to the picture's total statement, and what is the special function it must play? How warm or cool, how light or dark, how gray or intense is this particular red which he is counting on as an intrinsical part of his painting? Is it merely a thin, light tint or is it a saturated, rich, meaty red? These are some of the comparisons a painter must make and the questions he must ask himself as he builds with each and every color in his still life painting.

Having moved beyond the lay-in stage of the painting, it is no longer necessary for the sake of easier adjustments and control to continue to thin the pigment down with painting medium to the same extent as has been desirable up to this point. By using less medium and more pigment as one continues to construct the painting, the canvas will lend itself to greater variations of surface and become richer for the building of form.

One should always be involved with the more painterly aspects of the canvas, with the surface quality of the pigment itself, as it may contribute, through sensitive variation and changes of pace, to the greater fulfillment of his pictorial concept. The development of an artist's ability to handle the tools and media of his profession, in a personal and sensitive manner, must be the result of intimate involvement with his subject, and a direct outgrowth of his every response to this immediate experience.

Yes, one's ability to handle his media should become as personal as his signature. His manner of using pigment identifies him because it is the perfectly natural outgrowth of his development and experience as an artist. This is one of the many aspects of creative painting that ought not to be formalized or taught as a mannerism. All that an instructor should attempt in this area is to cultivate the student's awareness of the vast possibilities inherent in a genuinely painterly attitude. This, of course, will come about primarily through experience. Perhaps for a time it may become the student's self-conscious effort. But as he continues in creative work with his brush he will find that his use of a medium will become a natural and almost intuitive response. If his aesthetic awareness is given encouragement to grow in this manner, there will be little danger of his developing a manneristic technique of surface decoration.

And now he slowly builds his painting, moving back and forth throughout his canvas, through selectivity and sensitive adjustments, by elimination and addition, with concern always for the enrichment of the over-all concept; by pulling together these various elements that must function in a fully realized work of art, he should be well on his way in the development and completion of a still life painting.

In attempting to set down on paper the various fundamentals and steps that I feel are necessary in the entire growth of a painting, I recognize the danger that my teaching may seem over-intellectualized and somewhat academic. I do not offer what I have written as a formula or hard and fast rules that should never be violated. The painting fundamentals presented here are intended to serve only as additional tools to be used as the student finds his need for them. Tools will not, of course, guarantee successful painting, nor will they assure everyone of becoming a successful artist; but I have been urged to offer them because they have been used with success by my own pupils.

**Composing Around
A Central Image**

JAN STUSSY
White Flower with Black Leaves
Casein, 60 x 24
Courtesy Esther Robles Gallery

3 types
of composition

1 composing around a central theme

2 composing with a multiple view
   or variation of central image

3 the architectonic composition

The following three fundamental approaches to composition illustrated in this chapter are presented as suggestions for experimentation and are not intended as a comprehensive survey of the rich and varied range of design and composition.

The use of one central image as the basis for building a painting is deceptive in its apparent simplicity. This extreme limitation of subject matter demands that the negative areas or spaces that surround the image play a vital role in the over-all composition and are not simply left over to be arbitrarily filled in. The image and surrounding areas must be integrated in such a manner as to create a sense of the artist's total concern with the complete picture plane. The feeling of oneness, of being an entity.

The multiple view or variation of a central image opens up a wide range of possibilities for exploring various aspects of a single form and in turn building these many views into a cohesive structure or composition with each segment functioning and contributing to the construction of the total picture plane.

A more formal approach to design is the architectonic composition, in which the emphasis is placed upon the structural elements and aspects of the subject being painted, often resulting in a strong play against the horizontal and vertical planes of the canvas. The architectonic composition with its use of these structural aspects becomes unique by often being self-sufficient and frequently self-contained as though the design might well stand alone without the support of the canvas, very much like the building elements used in construction and architecture.

SUEO SERISAWA

Musical Instrument
Oil on canvas, 64 x 31
Courtesy Los Angeles County Museum

**Composing Around
Central Image**

DAN LUTZ

Fish Basket
Courtesy Dalzell Hatfield Galleries

Composing Around Central Image

BENTLEY SCHAAD
Orange Stump
Oil on canvas, 18 x 25
Courtesy Paul Rivas Gallery

Composing Around Central Image

JAMES JARVAISE
La Chambre
Oil on Masonite, 48 x 72
Courtesy Los Angeles County Museum
Junior Art Council Purchase Award, 1957

Variation of Central Image

WILLIAM BRICE
Rose Tree
Oil on canvas, 69 x 45
Courtesy Los Angeles County Museum
Gift of Jerome Shrbach

FLAVIA CABRAL

Four Shells

Oil, 14 x 32

Courtesy Dalzell Hatfield Galleries

Variation of Central Image

BENTLEY SCHAAD

Pomegranates
Oil on canvas, 25 x 36
Courtesy Paul Rivas Gallery

Variation of Central Image

ROGER KUNTZ
Morning Coffee
Courtesy Felix Landau Gallery

Composing with Architectonic Forms

PATRICIA J. BURG
Untitled
Mixed media on panel

Composing with Multiple View

BENTLEY SCHAAD
Skeletal Forms
Oil on canvas, 30 x 40
Courtesy Paul Rivas Gallery

Composing with Multiple View

Composing with Architectonic Forms

HELEN LUNDEBERG
Interior
Courtesy Paul Rivas Gallery

LENARD KESTER

The Parade
Oil on canvas, 24 x 29

Architectonic Composition

FREDERICK HAMMERSLEY
Growing Game
Oil on canvas, 40 x 30

Architectonic Composition

JOHN HULTBERG

Dark Coast

50 x 68

Courtesy Martha Jackson Gallery

Architectonic Composition

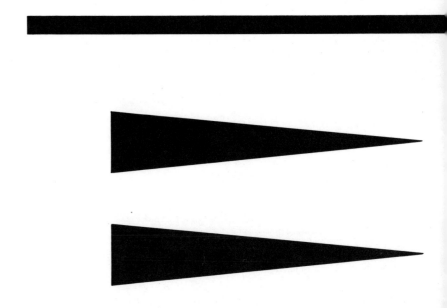

· G A L L E R Y ·

The following folio of paintings by a representative group of artists, all recognized as being among America's finest contemporary painters and draughtsmen, is presented as a cross-section of the magnificent scope and potential inherent in still life. It is not possible, within the space limitations of one book, to present all of the outstanding artists that have, from time to time, found still life a vital source of study and inspiration for truly important creative work. While this folio of paintings is by necessity limited in number, every effort has been made to select examples by brilliant artists that should help to illustrate the basic premise of this book: the realm of contemporary still life painting is limitless; that it is an exciting and a stimulating challenge for all artists. It is well to note that none of these artists should be identified as a "still life painter." In each case these men and women have distinguished themselves as artists greatly concerned and deeply involved with the full range of expression running from the figurative through abstraction, covering all areas and sources of inspiration. The illustrations of still life paintings by the late Henry Lee McFee are an excellent example of this. While McFee worked with still life material throughout his career and is often remembered chiefly for this one facet of his work,

his figure and landscape paintings are certainly among America's finest. There are many authorities who believe his painting Sleeping Black Girl to be one of the finest figure paintings ever produced in America.

Another interesting point to observe when reviewing this section is the wide variety of approaches and concepts employed by these artists in their use of still life material. Rarely is a table top used in what might be thought of as the conventional manner. One of the most important aspects of this folio, it seems to me, is that it clearly illustrates the great scope of painting and should totally destroy the cliché notion as to what constitutes a "still life." Often the most simple object or subject, through the skill and insight of these artists, is transformed into a meaningful and challenging statement in paint.

The artists represented have not been restricted in their comments or statements to still life painting; often both their comments and their painting illustrate their breadth of intellectual involvement and their concern for a greater understanding of the world in which they live. This in turn is reflected in their art regardless of the source of inspiration.

In painting I find landscape, figure, and still life equally interesting. In fact, I feel that almost any subject can present a challenge in which to find new visual dimensions. However, with landscape and figure there is always a sense of urgency brought about by the ever changing aspect of living things. On the other hand, still life gives the artist an opportunity for prolonged research with a controlled subject; thus he can study his subject without having to catch fragments bit by bit from the kaleidoscope of life. When I seek to expand my knowledge of spatial dimensions or experiment with new visual concepts, I turn to still life so that I can work without pressure.

I approach still life exactly as I approach all painting, making many free, exploratory sketches, researching the forms and the composition and becoming familiar with the actual physical shapes and their inter-relationship with the space and light around them. I also make quick color studies, usually in pastel or casein. In all of these I work directly from something that is real, letting the abstraction develop from the use of the medium and from the subject itself. This is a digestive process during which I work out inherited influences, divorce myself from representationalism and try to identify with the subject so that its forms take on a new meaning for me, and these shapes begin to arrange themselves in new compositional combinations. At this point I tack up on the wall all the sketches and paint-

ings I have done of the subject. I then study the sketches and prepare the canvas by underpainting. It is then that I am ready to paint.

The final painting is approached as a brand new adventure. I work quite fast so as not to lose the freshness of the painting, trying to keep a balance between reality and imagination. By this time I am so familiar with the subject that I no longer have to struggle with its physical realism and I am quite free to work with what I call the in-and-out structure of the spatial relationships, using the essence of the subject as a springboard and allowing the painting to grow from the facts that I have learned with my studies.

Each generation sees the ordinary sights of this world with new eyes. For instance we are creatures who travel across the earth's surface and above it at incredible speeds in the normal course of a day, so naturally our visual understanding of landscape is quite different from that of our grandparents' who rode slowly across its surface in animal drawn vehicles. Is it any wonder, then, that contemporary men demand a different pictorial representation of earth and its objects than did our ancestors? This is why in recent years, along with looking for new and exciting subject matter in the incunabula of our time, I often choose still life subjects that have become known as trite and conventional, such as old bottles, fruit or flowers and try to revitalize my vision on these subjects.

JAE CARMICHAEL

JAE CARMICHAEL
Fall Bouquet
Oil on canvas

RICHARD HAINES
Possessions
Oil on canvas, 28 x 44
Courtesy Dalzell Hatfield Galleries

I have always been interested in painting things—people, rocks, boats, machines, plants, etc. I have not been concerned with painting these objects for their interest alone but, rather, for what they can be made to imply or reveal. My principal concern is the drama of man and his environment. I believe a painting is an independent object, an event, a thing of personality, with various levels of communication; the contents corresponding to the intensity of the subjective experience that initiated it.

I want a painting to have a strong image with a particular kind of emotion and I strive for a tension between mystery and fact, space and substance, attitude and objectivity. I hope for the painting to be alive and have a rewarding experience for the viewer.

Regarding **Copper Country**, it's a kind of a "ghost town" idea—and as for the painting **Possessions** it was inspired by the very private collection of objects, things, mementos, that people sometimes save.

RICHARD HAINES

RICHARD HAINES

Copper Country

Oil on canvas, 36 x 48

Courtesy Dalzell Hatfield Galleries

Of all the many problems in the art of painting, the problem of Space seems to me the most central and important. To me it is a matter of a painter's personal temperament and inclination whether he chooses to stress color, design, or form in his painting; whether his work is essentially emotional, intellectual or factual; whether it be representational or non-objective. However, the artist's attitude toward space and his treatment of it underlies his painting in any of these categories.

Perhaps space is a problem because it cannot be represented directly; it can only be expressed indirectly by means of forms, shapes, .colors and lines, which through their inter-relations, delimit and define it. Hence it is not surprising that it should be elusive, even somewhat mystical. Nor is it surprising to me that many artists have dealt with it in an intuitive way. Not all artists however. The Cubist movement, fathered by Braque and Picasso, was essentially an attempt to subject the space problem to rigid discipline and control. Likewise, the Renaissance development with its use of perspective, both linear and atmospheric, was essentially a deliberate discipline. The basic distinction between these two movements lies in their differing attitudes toward space,

hence in a changed technique and esthetic.

The cubists quickly learned that the most obvious, possibly the best and perhaps the only way to deal with the matter was by stressing the importance of the picture plane as a frame of reference to which all movement in depth should be related. By now this concept of the picture plane (as represented by the canvas surface) has rather completely permeated and influenced all subsequent painting, whether representational, abstract or non-objective. The painter today has a heightened awareness, a developed sensitivity regarding the preservation of his picture surface. He has learned that a spot of color must stay on the surface, at the same time expressing the third dimensional movement into depth.

Merely preserving the picture plane, however, does not necessarily, or automatically, produce good art. It is a means, a tool, not an end in itself. It can be used in various ways. Chirico, for instance, tried, and in his better canvases succeeded, in preserving his picture plane while stretching space in depth, thereby creating an almost unbearable feeling of nostalgic solitude and melancholy. On the other hand, most non-objective painters of today compress and contract the third dimension, the picture's depth, al-

most out of existence. I say "almost" because with the good men of this school it is a question of extreme or subtle compression and not of elimination. They want the subject—or the lack of it—in any case the content of their painting to become identified completely with the physical canvas; to do this they relate all depth-sense to the picture plane. Only through relation to this frame of reference does any depth feeling have significance.

Another matter that interests me is the degree to which we are all unconsciously moved by the sense of space. In the work of Chirico just mentioned, it seems obvious that it is the distortion or manipulation of space that produces the emotional reaction. What, then, is our unconscious emotional reaction to the extreme contraction of the depth element? In the early days of the modern movement, when distorted drawing stirred the wrath of the general public, was the painter really trying to distort space to attain his effect, finding it necessary to distort objects in the process? And finally, in non-objective painting today, is the antagonism of many people due not to the absence of representation, as they think, but rather to their unconscious reaction to an unfamiliar, and hence highly disturbing, treatment of space?
Russell Cowles

RUSSELL COWLES
Pine Branches
Oil on canvas, 40 x 50

Courtesy Dalzell Hatfield Galleries

KERO ANTOYAN
Melons
Oil on Masonite, 22 x 34
Collection of the Artist

For some, actual realism is essential.
For me, the essence of the melon is
more important than the image.
Each slice, each different cut, gives
me the feeling of the true tender
sweetness and the velvety texture of
the melons, and provides me with a
point of departure into inventive
shapes which transform the subject
as they reveal its true essence.
White on White (See page 70.)
This is one of my early paintings.
It shows my reverence for whiteness
as a theme. I chose to use a semi-
abstract approach, and attempted to
treat the subject with intellectual
understanding of the visual reality.

KERO ANTOYAN

I have always felt an affinity with subject matter. I cannot deny the world about us, even its smallest aspect—hence, still life has always fascinated me. It is a symbol of painting for itself, a complete statement for the painter. Out of the mundane and humble can emerge something elegant and noble with the impact of a gong.

Subject or nature is inherent. We live in it, it engulfs us, so we are saturated in it and know it best. A painter must paint with love and fire or not at all, and for the simple and sheer joy of painting and not necessarily for exhibition or prestige, for the moment ego or the desire for applause enters into his consciousness he becomes a charlatan, or an actor out of his right place.

But the message of the painter is expression and freedom born out of discipline, craftsmanship, and meditation. If his talent is sufficient, his vision beyond the obvious, and his heart in his work, he will make contact. Others will share his joy and excitement at the moment of doing. Everything the artist is is poured into this intense moment, the act of painting. So the artist must first deal with himself, for he finds painting not only his outlet but proof of himself.

Painting as an art is a way of life. One's whole being necessarily rotates around it. An artist lives forever with his work. It is a total concentration of everything one is, or at least capable of being, in one concentrated effort—and to me the intensity of the moment is very important. It is like the rays of the sun projected through a magnifying glass into a pin point of light on one particular object. The bare canvas and the artist come into contact, and through this creative concentration, through this projection of himself he raises his dead canvas to something alive and part of him. He must imbue it with life from himself else he has failed. With this must come great enthusiasm, an arrogant humility, as total an awareness as is possible, and the seeking for the freedom of choice at his disposal—yet everything embodied in the obviously limited means, for by the very limitation of the medium the viewer reacts and this gives painting its dignity and power. Without the sensitive viewer a painting is like a play which has never been acted on a stage, or a symphony never heard, for it lives only through the one who sees it.

We never do all that we are really capable of doing. Anybody who has thought seriously for a moment would not deny this. But the full potential of this is wonderfully present when the painter faces his canvas, the sculptor his stone or clay, the writer his blank sheets of paper. The artist must love, and above all he must love his work and be aware of a presence inside that says: I am here now, I am free to do this now because I so desire with real intensity, and I have worked and struggled to be capable of doing this—now I do. We are all little in this world and this universe. Of all the acts that make one transcend this littleness is the awareness of our own personal idiom, our own expression, and of doing something we think important.

ROBERT FRAME

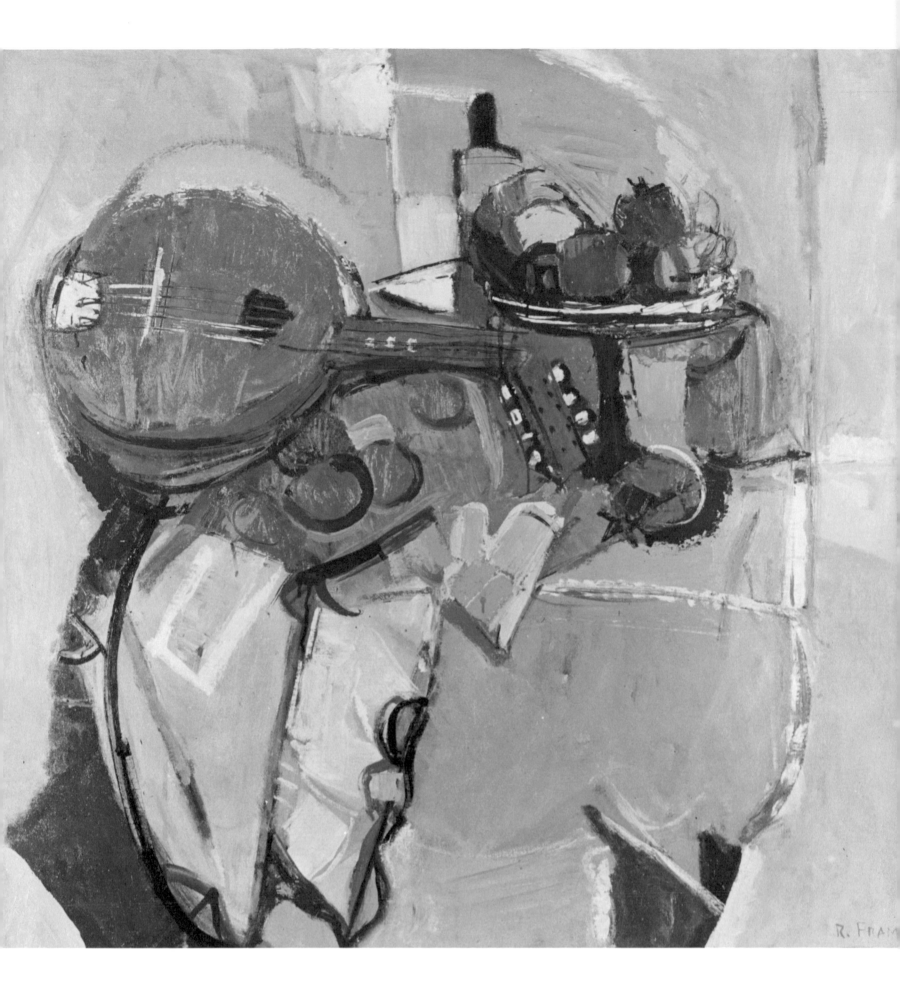

ROBERT CHUEY
The White Pitcher
Collection City Art Museum of St. Louis
Gift of Mr. Morton May

To quicken the inanimate.

To render a mystical (I use the word with a certain reservation) existence to these forgotten objects. The still life moves as a sumptuous cortege emulating the classic and the quaint with its strange energies. It is always there, waiting, anticipating, enigmatic.

The still life has an independent nature. It ignores the moralizing and psychological implications necessary to a didactic work. However, the still life can be deeply incisive in humanistic terms.

For these objects are human wrought, symbolically alive and organic—subsequently, the human experience can be read on them. One need only see again Goya, Soutine, Rembrandt, Van Gogh, Rouault, Picasso.

For myself, painting relates more deeply to music than to literature. To deal with the image in literary terms is perhaps more challenging because of history. And in this area there are much fewer really eloquent practitioners. In the pictures reproduced here the dramatic sequence of objects and cast shadows seems to form a strong basis for composing which particularly interests me. An interexchange of energies and cause and effect relationships weave and work together with a certain inevitability. Perhaps this gives emphasis to the metaphysical condition of the object. Thus I see the still life as deeply personal and eternal.

ROBERT CHUEY

ROBERT CHUEY
Untitled
Collection of Mr. Vincent Price

Painting has been my dominant interest since childhood. I have generally wished to develop drawings and paintings that have a sense of movement as opposed to a static quality. Any subject or idea which I find stimulating aesthetically is used as a point of departure and to this I graft my previous knowledge, experiences, and emotions in painting and living, so that each work for better or worse is always at least one thing—a reflection of its creator.

Still life as subject matter is one of the best means of expressing the unity in variety for which all art strives. In **Curio Collection** I have used a combination of natural and man-made objects grouped together in a semi-abstract arrangement with planes arbitrarily placed to develop a sense of movement and a flickering, patterned effect. In this painting color, shape, and texture play more important roles than form, as I desired to keep the picture plane quite flat.

JEAN JOURDAIN

JEAN JOURDAIN
Curio Collection
Oil on canvas, 20 x 25

DOUGLAS McCLELLAN
Still Life
Courtesy Felix Landau Gallery

Painting in our age has become one of the last outposts of the individual statement. I feel that this is unfortunate in that it has sensitized artists to the manufacture of "individual statements" and in so doing has reduced uniqueness to an indulgent exercise.

Working as I do from some visual or literary motif outside of the painting, I try to be moved by the motif, trusting that my response and the resulting forms cannot help but be my own. My recent paintings have been concerned with objects as generalized forms that have the power to present an evocative image. I hope that they can express much to the viewer that is valid to him without distracting his attention to the artist, who is really no longer a necessary party in the communication.

DOUGLAS McCLELLAN

I came to know that it was not the well realized objects that made the picture compelling, but rather the significant way the canvas was put together. I sensed a life of the forms that was not always the result of vision but rather a clearer understanding of the motif. When we think of the motif, that particular piece or section of the visual world that we have under consideration, we must realize that the spaces are as important as the objects, and remember that we have the problem of making of that which is before us a living plastic unit of design. If we can organize our efforts and get beneath the surface—find out what is really significant to us—we have a chance of making the picture live. I once had the experience of suddenly perceiving in my garden with its

HENRY LEE McFEE
Still Life—Oranges
Oil on canvas, 40 x 30
Courtesy Whitney Museum of American Art

familiar background of trees and sky the overpowering design that explained the whole. It was as if the very spirit of the motif projected itself.

Sometimes we can sense at once what will be the dominant organic rhythm of the emotional form of the complex material before us. At other times it is by experimenting and analyzing that we arrive at the certainty of what is right. This certainty we must have. The painter may be interested in the architectonic qualities alone or he may desire to realize as well something of the richness, fullness, and glory of the visual world. The essential thing is that the completed picture shall be a living unit of design, strong in tactile values and plastic in every sense. From the late Henry McFee's writings.

ARNOLD SCHIFRIN
Smelts
Oil on canvas, 14 x 18
Collection Mr. and Mrs. Charles Lewis

It is so simple, what I believe my art should be that I wonder why it is so hard for me to attain. That the painting would show my response to the objects I paint—that this be my "style"—that the only true style be from the understanding of the artist. A painting tells me as much of the painter as of the painting.

I come from a draughtsman's school, Delacroix, Rubens, Goya, Daumier; so gesture becomes much to me. As I paint and my sympathy grows, I will arbitrarily heighten colors, accent lines to declare myself with the clarity and force I feel necessary. I have given up the thought of doing a delicate painting—my effects are broad, large, and sensuous. This suits my nature best. That is my response to life at my most profound.

I seem to learn by drawing—much more than by talking. My eyes speak to me—I have learned to trust them, to pick out the important parts. Always I would want my art to return us full circle to life, more prepared to live, richer than before. I am not of the school of studio pictures. It is an interplay between life and art —each helping the other as one falters.   ARNOLD SCHIFRIN

Beauty and truth are the absolutes which guide my approach to painting. I believe that the pursuit of these absolutes and the fulfillment of them in any creative manner is an achievement of eternal significance. To my mind the measure of the artist is in direct proportion to how forcefully, brilliantly, naïvely, and consciously or unconsciously he has imbued the work with his own spirit or being. I work intuitively in whichever medium or manner appeals to me at the moment.

JAMES STROMBOTNE

JAMES STROMBOTNE

Still Life with Self Portrait

Oil on canvas, 50 x 44

Courtesy Frank Perls Gallery

WALTER ASKIN
Classic Flowering
Oil on canvas, 68 x 46

The following four terms describe the principal characteristics of my concerns in painting:

Comprehensive: The purpose of painting is to connect a variety of experiences into a significant whole.

Paintings are valuable to the degree they are concerned with realities, not abstractions. An abstraction is an understandable unit of reality emphasizing a segment of the creative being. It is a move in the direction of simple primitivism, purity, therapy, protective security, and refers to artificial limits. Paintings concerned with the nature of reality move toward increasing complexity, increased awareness, the demands of life, and the development toward ultimates. The immediate past history of painting is the development of purism of all kinds. It is also a period of emerging freedom of choice for the individual; barriers are broken down; substitute limitations are created. Puristic painting makes a part the whole; comprehensive painting develops a whole consisting of parts. Comprehensive painting demands an artist be concerned with realities, with the totality of existence, with the totality of experience.

Developmental: The procedure in painting is the search for a relationship of parts.

The history of the progress of man is the record of his ability to make connections. The job of the painter today is to pull together simple, specialized, pure, primitive directions into a work allowing all elements to merge—associations, emotional connotations, fantasies, remembered perceptions, remembered paintings of the artist and others in the stream of history, and any other imagery coming to mind at the time of painting. Instead of recording a conclusion, the process of painting is an active and lively experience for the artist. If the process of creating a work is magic, the result will be magic. Is this random and playful? It may be that the reasons for being exist in such procedures. In this kind of act, painting becomes not a recapitulation of experience but a unique addition to experience.

Relative: The meaning of painting is found in the kind of relationship established between its qualities.

Quality in a work of art is an equation of quantities. Therefore, a primary interest of the painter is in the principle of balance. The other old principles of art (proportion, rhythm, subordination, opposition, transition) are simply attributes of balance. When parts are brought into unity, into balance, there is a reaction making the whole greater in force than the sum of the parts. As the number of associations, connections outside the painting, and suggestions of other experiences increases, the meaning of the work becomes mature. The deeper the meaning the closer the painting comes to having a sense of reality, truth, authority. Conjectural elements are presented in a state of equivocation true to their nature, not as absolutes.

Natural: The means of establishing a synergetic whole in painting is the natural unity of the individual human being.

The basic premise in painting is a belief in the nature of man and his ability to develop a real, or truthful, or fit, or proper, or meaningful, or significant relationship of his total experience. The objective is a multivalent work allowing the artist to sum up his whole being in the act of painting.
WALTER ASKIN

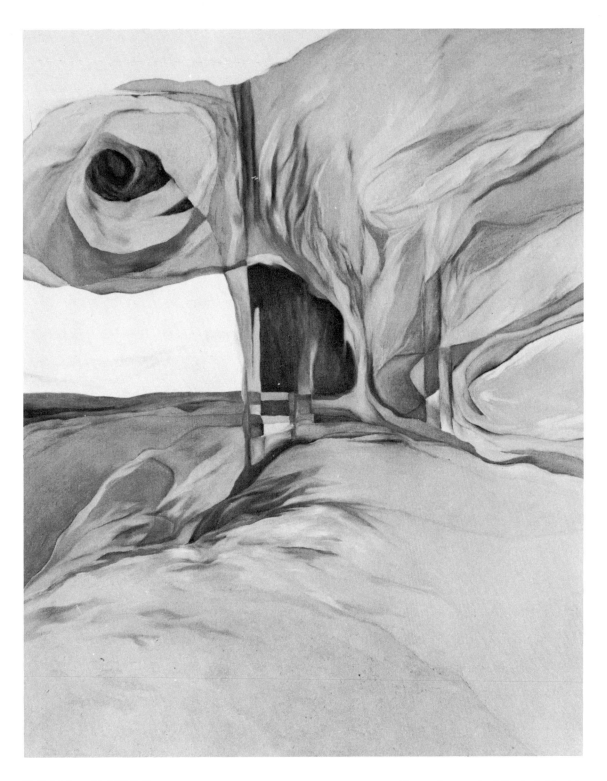

PAUL RIVAS
Background Plant Forms
Collection, Mr. Larry Urrutia

The environment of the individual is a many-sided one. The world of the outside is ever present—the far away, quiet, green scene. The interior becomes one with the outside world of nature. At every living moment all exists within: the leaf, the ocean, the table, the road, the fabric, the cloud, the background, the fear, the foreground, the love, the hope, the tragedy. To express the whole entity of one human is my idea. To suggest thoughts that lead and become entangled with other entities and form an experience is my idea. A communication within souls.
PAUL RIVAS

PAUL DARROW
Shore Still Life
Courtesy Comara Gallery

I have always been attracted by the shapes of discarded, abandoned, broken tools and materials of civilization. Rusting machinery; airplane, automotive, and marine wreckage seem more real and expressive than their well-ordered and functioning counterparts.

I have often been asked about my choice of subject matter, my preoccupation with ruin and decay. My work doesn't consciously express social protest, propaganda, superficial message, or obvious symbolism. Most artists are teased by particular subjects and shapes. I find unexpected and exciting combinations of shapes, patterns, and textures in crushed metal, splintered wood, tangled iron, rotting pilings. Often I make detailed sketches of these arrangements. Working in the studio, the sketch is soon absorbed in a new involvement of canvas and paint. The initial impulse, the remembered scene, and the emotions crowd in. The painting is a new thing when finished—a combination of the scene, the sketch, and the artist's involvement.

Wreckage, pilings, and flotsam pushed together by the sea and stranded by the tide were the motivation of **Shore Still Life.**
PAUL DARROW

HANS BURKHARDT
Love of Two Nails
Oil on canvas, 32 x 42
Courtesy Ankrum Gallery

My ideas for paintings come from many things, such as the tortured wires and rusty nails of a city dump; the happy play, as well as the sad faces of children; dogs dying on a Mexican street; wars, political upheavals.

Sometimes I am concerned with interpreting a mood, an idea, and find that only the abstract or non-objective will serve my purpose. At other times I am concerned with the visual or material aspect of a subject and feel the need for a more realistic or semi-abstract approach.

Painting to me is a way of expressing all that life holds for me, all that life means to me, as well as a groping for clarification of all the things not quite fathomed, but dimly sensed. The most important thing is that whatever I express in my painting must be born out of my deepest convictions and must satisfy me, if it satisfies no one else.

HANS BURKHARDT